GW00500258

THE

Little Book

— OF —

BUDDHIST WISDOM

THE
Little Book
— OF —
BUDDHIST WISDOM

Compiled by
RICHARD AND DIANA ST. RUTH

ELEMENT

Shaftesbury, Dorset ◆ Rockport, Massachusetts
Brisbane, Queensland

© ELEMENT BOOKS LIMITED 1997

Published in Great Britain in 1997 by
ELEMENT BOOKS LIMITED
Shaftesbury, Dorset SP7 9BP

Published in the USA in 1997 by
ELEMENT BOOKS, INC.
PO Box 830, Rockport, MA 01966

Published in Australia in 1997 by
ELEMENT BOOKS LIMITED
for JACARANDA WILEY LIMITED
33 Park Road, Milton, Brisbane 4064

Cover illustration: Tangku hanging temple picture, 18th century

Designed by
BRIDGEWATER BOOKS

Printed and bound in Italy by Imago
British Library Cataloguing in Publication data available
Library of Congress Cataloging in Publication data available

ISBN 1 86204 055 9

The publishers would like to thank the following for the use of pictures:

e.t. archive

INTRODUCTION

The Buddha was a man who woke up to the truth — the word 'buddha' means 'to have awoken.' He realized why beings suffer and how to come away from that suffering.

The Buddha's teaching was, therefore, based on each person experiencing the truth of suffering and the ending of suffering for themselves. It is simple and obvious as well as profound and mysterious. The essence of his teaching can be summed up in the following four truths:

I. THE TRUTH OF SUFFERING: To face the reality of our own suffering. A distinction is drawn here between physical pain and mental suffering. Suffering in Buddhist terms means anguish, heartache, longing, wishing, hoping for a person or an object or a condition which is not present.

II. THE TRUTH OF THE CAUSE OF SUFFERING: To acknowledge the fact that we suffer because we don't like what we have; we desire things to be different from how they actually are. Desire itself is then seen to be the root cause of suffering rather than the inability to achieve the object of our desires.

III. THE TRUTH OF THE CESSATION OF SUFFERING: To realize that, by resisting the pull to desire things, suffering ceases. To experience this as a reality is called nirvana – the cooling of the heat of wanting and anguishing.

IV. THE TRUTH OF THE WAY OF LIFE THAT IS FREE OF SUFFERING: To live in a manner which values the moment as it is, is free of desire, and free of suffering in oneself. This is a totally harmless way of life and benefits all beings. It is generally presented as the noble eightfold path: right view, intention, speech, action, livelihood, effort, mindfulness, concentration.

The following extracts and sayings will give the reader a taste of Buddhism. The attempt has been made to draw from all the traditions which have developed over the centuries right back to the Buddha himself, who lived two and a half thousand years ago.

It is suggested that each page be taken one at a time, rather than read straight through as a book. Each piece can be quietly reflected upon. It will then work for you and bring spiritual happiness and nourishment.

May all beings be well and happy.

RICHARD AND DIANA ST. RUTH

People ask me what my religion is.
I tell them, 'My religion is kindness.'

TENZIN GYATSO
His Holiness the 14th Dalai Lama

● ● ●

The foolish believe that their
own interests will suffer
if they put the benefits of others first.

DOGEN
Japanese Zen Master, 1200–1253

The more we take the welfare
of others to heart and work for their benefit,
the more benefit we derive for ourselves.
This is a fact that we can see.

And the more selfish we remain and
self-centred, the more selfish our way of life is,
the lonelier we feel and the more miserable.
This is also a fact that we can see.

TENZIN GYATSO
His Holiness the 14th Dalai Lama

When selfishness really hurts,

then the path is easy.

Zen Graffiti

In the religious life,

never take leave of good sense.

PHIROZ MEHTA
Buddhist scholar, 1902–1994

Act so that you have no cause to be
ashamed of yourselves; and hold fast to this rule.

JETSUN MILAREPA
Tibetan Buddhist yogi, 1025–1135

● ● ●

Let no one think lightly of evil,
thinking – 'It will not touch me.'
Drop by drop is a water pot filled;
little by little the fool becomes filled with evil.

Dhammapada, verse 121

How can there be laughter and joy when the
world is always burning?
Enveloped in darkness,
why do you not seek the light?

Dhammapada, verse 146

● ● ●

The stones which were thrown at me –
When I picked it up,
one of them was a jewel.

Japanese poem

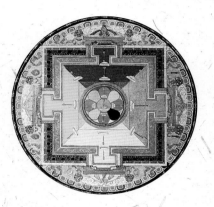

A team of the fastest horses cannot over-
take a word once it has left the lips.

Old Chinese saying

The perfect way is difficult
only for those who pick and choose…

MASTER SENG-T'SAN
third patriarch of Chinese Ch'an/Zen, d.606

For those with preferences,
suffering is inevitable.

AJAHN BRAHMAMUNI
Thai monk

The Great Way is serene and all-embracing,

in it nothing is easy, nothing is difficult;

partial views – doubtful and insecure –

at times run riot and are very prone to cling.

MASTER SENG-T'SAN
third patriarch of Chinese Ch'an/Zen, d.606

● ● ●

Eighty percent is perfect!

Zen saying

The past should not be followed after,

the future not desired.

What is past is got rid of

and the future has not come.

But whoever has vision now here,

now there, of a present thing,

knowing that it is immovable, unshakeable,

let him cultivate it.

Swelter at the task this very day.

Who knows whether he will die tomorrow?

There is no bargaining with

the great hosts of Death.

BUDDHA

Try not to live as if time were a reality
which can steal away your life.

Life is short,
yet the moment transcends eternity.

Zen Graffiti

Whatever is past is past, so do not sit
in judgement upon it. Whatever is in the future
is not here yet, so do not direct your
hopes and longings towards it.

HUI HAI
Chinese Ch'an / Zen Master, 720–814

★ 19 ★

Even though the body may yield to death,
the mind in a state of nirvana
does not die.

BUDDHADASA BHIKKHU
Thai meditation monk

That which ye sow ye reap.

See yonder fields!

The sesamum was sesamum,

the corn was corn.

The Silence and the Darkness knew!

So is a man's fate born.

SIR EDWIN ARNOLD
The Light of Asia

The way is perfect and complete
like boundless space;
nothing is lacking, nothing redundant,
but, because the mind continues
to make distinctions,
its suchness is obscured.

MASTER SENG-T'SAN
third patriarch of
Chinese Ch'an / Zen, d. 606

That which comes in through the
front door is not the family treasure.

Zen saying

A foolish passing thought
makes one an ordinary man,
while an enlightened second thought
makes one a buddha.

MASTER HUI NENG
sixth patriarch of Chinese Ch'an / Zen, 638–713

As a solid rock is not shaken by the wind,

even so are the wise unshaken

by blame or praise.

Dhammapada, verse 81

Even as the light of a lamp can

break up darkness

which has been there for a thousand years,

so a spark of wisdom can do away with ignorance

which has lasted for ages.

MASTER HUI NENG

sixth patriarch of Chinese Ch'an / Zen, 638–713

Buddh, who wept with all my brothers' tears,
whose heart was broken by a whole world's woe,
laugh and am glad, for there is liberty!
Ho! Ye who suffer! Know

ye suffer from yourselves. None else compels,
none other holds you that ye live and die,
and whirl upon the wheel,
and hug and kiss its spokes of agony...

SIR EDWIN ARNOLD
The Light of Asia

If one can, during the morning and evening,
keep the heart completely without
differentiation whether walking, standing,
sitting, or reclining, this will then be the
manifestation of a buddha.

It is not necessary to use the mind or
to employ one's strength, or to produce or
construct anything. One should not trouble
oneself with the least chatter or contemplation.
Therefore, we say, to achieve buddhahood is
the simplest of things!

MASTER HSU YUN
Chinese Ch'an

Where one has awoken
to the sameness of everything,
there is the great enlightenment.

VAIROCANA
a symbolic buddha, Mahayana school

Refrain from all evil,

do what is good,

cleanse your own thoughts.

This is the advice of the buddhas.

Dhammapada, verse 183

Mind, Buddha and living beings do not

differ from one another.

HUI HAI

Chinese Ch'an/Zen Master, 720–814

Whosoever says that the Tathagata* goes or comes, stands, sits or lies down, he does not understand the meaning of my teaching. And why? 'Tathagata' is called one who has not gone anywhere, nor come from anywhere. Therefore is he called 'the Tathagata, the Arhat, the fully Enlightened One'.

BUDDHA

* The Buddha referred to himself as the Tathagata, a word meaning 'thus come', 'the one who neither comes nor goes'.

t is through your own bodies

that reality is perceived;

the Buddha is perceived in the same manner.

VIMALAKIRTI
layman at the time of the Buddha
Mahayana school

Is material shape permanent

or impermanent?

Impermanent, revered sir.

But is what is impermanent painful or pleasant?

Painful, revered sir.

And is it right to regard

that which is impermanent, suffering,

liable to change, as

'This is mine, this am I, this is my self'?

No, revered sir.

BUDDHA
speaking to his monks

Whatever is material shape,
past, future, present, subjective or objective,
gross or subtle, mean or excellent,
whether it is far or near — all material shape
should be seen by perfect intuitive wisdom as it
really is: 'This is not mine, this am I not,
this is not my self.'

BUDDHA

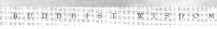

Yuan once asked: Do you make efforts
in your practice of the Way, Master?

Hui Hai: Yes, I do.

Yuan: How?

Hui Hai: When hungry, I eat;

when tired, I sleep.

Yuan: And does everybody make
the same efforts as you do, Master?

Hui Hai: Not in the same way.

Yuan: Why not?

Hui Hai: When they are eating, they think of a
hundred kinds of necessities, and when they are
going to sleep, they ponder over affairs of a
thousand different kinds.

That is how they differ from me.

HUI HAI
Chinese Ch'an/Zen Master, 720–814

All wisdom comes from the essence of

mind and not from an exterior source.

Have no mistaken notion about that.

This is called 'Self use of the true nature.'

MASTER HUI NENG

sixth patriarch of Chinese Ch'an / Zen, 638–713

There is an unborn, an unbecome,

an unmade, an unformed.

If there was not an unborn,

there could be no escape from what is born.

But since there is an unborn,

there is an escape.

BUDDHA

Who would have thought that the essence of mind is intrinsically pure!
Who would have thought that the essence of mind is intrinsically free from becoming or annihilation!
Who would have thought that the essence of mind is intrinsically self sufficient!
Who would have thought that the essence of mind is intrinsically free from change!
Who would have thought that all things are the manifestation of the essence of mind!

MASTER HUI NENG

sixth patriarch of Chinese Ch'an/Zen, 638–713

Here, from the very beginning, there is this
One Thing.

Constantly lucid and mysterious,

it has never been born and it has never died.

It cannot be named or depicted.

SOSAN
Korean Son/Zen Grand Master, 1520–1604

Siddhartha Gautama* –

born a long time ago,

died a long time ago.

Buddha – never born, never died.

Zen Graffiti

* Siddhartha Gautama was the family name of the man who became
the Buddha.

Those who see into their true nature,
are instantaneously initiated into
all the mystic teachings.

Zen Graffiti

SOURCES AND ACKNOWLEDGEMENTS

Pp.7B, 8T, 20: *Buddhism Now* magazine. Copyright © Buddhist Publishing Group, Totnes, Devon. Pp.10T, 18T, 44,46: *Zen Graffiti*, Azuki. Copyright © 1991 Buddhist Publishing Group, Totnes, Devon. P.11T: *Introduction to Buddhism*. Copyright © 1988 Diana St. Ruth. Buddhist Publishing Group, Totnes, Devon. Pp.11B, 12T, 27T, 32T: Books consulted: *Dhammapada*, translated by E.W. Adikaram. Copyright © 1954 M.D. Gunasena & Co. Ltd, Colombo, and *Dhammapada*. Copyright © Jack Austin 1945. The Buddhist Society, London. P.12B: *Fingers & Moons*. Copyright © 1988 Trevor Leggett. Buddhist Publishing Group, Totnes, Devon. Pp.14T, 15T, 23: *On Trust in the Heart and Believing in Mind, Hsin Hsin Ming*. Attributed to Seng-t'san, third patri- arch of Ch'an, a rendering by Eric Turner 1982. Buddhist Publishing Group, Totnes, Devon. P.14B: *The Burdened Heart*, Ajahn Brahmamuni. Translated by Ajahn Sumedho. Copyright © 1984 Buddhist Publishing Group, Totnes, Devon. P.17: *Lomasakangiya on the Auspicious* from *The Collection of The Middle Length Sayings (Majjhima-Nikaya)*, Vol. III. Translated from the Pali by I.B. Horner. Copyright © 1959 The Pali Text Society, Oxford. P.35: *Greater Discourse (at the time) of a Full Moon (Mahapunnamasutta)* from *The Collection of The Middle Length Sayings*